NEW TESTAMENT SYMBOLS

TOPIC 1 –
New Testament Symbols

Key Points

- The Old Covenant is characterised by religious symbols which God used to express spiritual principles. Some symbols are easily understood and others less so. But all symbols were given for a purpose.

- The dispensation of the church is characterised by a lack of symbolism and a stronger focus on personal righteousness.

- The assemblies described in the N.T. had no sacred buildings, altars, gorgeous robes, religious festivals or any of the physical accompaniments of the Old Covenant.

- Christendom has retained and adapted many of the symbols of the Old Covenant as well as adding a host of new symbols.

The Purpose of Symbols

The world is full of symbols. The crown on the king's head is a symbol of his authority. The white wedding gown of the bride is a symbol of her purity. The lion rampant symbolises Scotland and the dragon symbolises Wales. Symbols abound. But what exactly is a symbol? It is difficult to come up with a comprehensive definition but essentially a symbol is an object or act that represents or stands for something else. Here are some other illustrations. The sergeant wears three stripes on his shoulder to symbolize his rank. The courtier bends his knee and the lady in waiting curtsies to the queen. These acts symbolise deference to her authority.

In these studies we will look at the symbols found in the New Testament. In order to keep the study manageable we will not look at symbolic language e.g. "I am the bread of life" or "I am the door" but at acts or objects which have symbolic meaning.

The Prominence of Symbols
Christendom is replete with religious symbols. Crucifixes often with a representation of the Lord Jesus are displayed prominently in buildings or worn on chains round the neck. Many attach the symbol of a fish to their lapels or bible bags (the *icthus*). Bishops carry croziers and wear miters. Christianity seems to be a religion of symbols.

In fact the N.T. has very little teaching about symbolism. The only symbols prescribed are baptism for believers, bread and wine at the Lord's Supper and the prescriptions in connection with head covering in First Corinthians ch 11.

It is interesting to note that prior to the giving of the Law there were only a handful of religious symbols mandated by God e.g. circumcision (Gen. 17:11). The N.T. teaches that it has been superseded and is now redundant (Acts 15:1, 5, 24; 1 Cor. 7:19). The pre-Sinai sacrifices, seem to have been commanded by God (e.g. Gen. 4:4; 8:20) although there is little in the way of detail. But although the Patriarchs engaged in symbolic activity e.g. Gen. 24:2; 28:18, religious activity prior to the Law was not characteristically symbolic. The only symbol pre-dating the Law that survives today is a symbol God gave to all humanity - the rainbow (Gen. 9:12-13). Initially given to Noah, it is a symbol of God's promise not to flood the earth again.

This is in marked contrast to the profusion of symbols that were given to Israel after they left Egypt and entered into the Covenant of Law at Sinai. The furniture of the tabernacle, the sacrifices, the garments of the High Priest, the religious festivals and Levitical offerings are all part of a lengthy list of symbols required by Jehovah. The materials used, the design, the shape and function all had symbolic meaning. The Law was a religion laden with symbolic rite and ritual.

The Passing of Symbols
The N.T. teaches that the religious symbols of the Old Covenant were transitory and designed to point forward to the substance (Col. 2:16). With the advent of Christ the need for symbols passed away. Hence in the New Testament epistles Paul does not teach that Christians should have altars or incense, temples or robes, feasts or rituals. All of these things have been superseded by Christ (Heb. 10:1). Nor did the Lord or the apostles introduce new Christian rites and ordinances to replace those provided by the Law. Hence there is no warrant in

scripture for Christian feasts or holy days. There is no Shrove Tuesday or Ash Wednesday. No sign of the cross or rosary. No candles or incense.

The religion of the N.T. is predominantly a matter of the heart and spirit. It does not depend on performance of rites or rituals. While true religion finds physical expression in good deeds, physical purity, hymns of praise and the spoken word, it is not defined by these things. They are or may be its manifestations. For this reason it is noteworthy that the spread of the gospel and the establishment of the assemblies did not involve that which appeals to our physical senses. Incense, stained glass windows or spectacular architecture belong to the era of Law. Music was a prominent feature of Temple worship (e.g. 1 Chron. 15:16; 23:5) but the assembly gatherings of the N.T. do not involve musical instruments of any sort nor do the apostles give any guidance on musical accompaniment. The trumpets, cymbals and harps (Ps. 150) give way to psalms, hymns and spiritual songs (Eph. 5:19; Col. 3:16). The N.T. describes a simple, unvarnished form of worship. The most prosaic explanation for this is that the assemblies had been cut off from the Temple with its elaborate instrumentation and had neither the means or resources to supply themselves with trumpets or cymbals. However there is a more profound explanation for this change. The absence of instrumentation is in harmony with a general move away from that which is sensory to that which is spiritual. It may therefore be inferred that the unaccompanied singing of the N.T. is normative for the Church age.

 ## KEY SCRIPTURES

20 Our fathers worshipped in this mountain; and ye say, that in Jerusalem is the place where men ought to worship. 21 Jesus saith unto her, Woman, believe me, the hour cometh, when ye shall neither in this mountain, nor yet at Jerusalem, worship the Father. 22 Ye worship ye know not what: we know what we worship: for salvation is of the Jews. 23 But the hour cometh, and now is, when the true worshippers shall worship the Father in spirit and in truth: for the Father seeketh such to worship him. 24 God *is* a Spirit: and they that worship him must worship *him* in spirit and in truth.

Jn 4:20-24

KEY SCRIPTURES

[3] For we are the circumcision, which worship God in the spirit, and rejoice in Christ Jesus, and have no confidence in the flesh.

Phil 3:3

[16] Let no man therefore judge you in meat, or in drink, or in respect of an holyday, or of the new moon, or of the sabbath *days*: [17] Which are a shadow of things to come; but the body *is* of Christ.

Col 2:16-17

[1] For the law having a shadow of good things to come, *and* not the very image of the things, can never with those sacrifices which they offered year by year continually make the comers thereunto perfect. [2] For then would they not have ceased to be offered? because that the worshippers once purged should have had no more conscience of sins. [3] But in those *sacrifices there* is a remembrance again *made* of sins every year. [4] For *it is* not possible that the blood of bulls and of goats should take away sins.

Heb 10:1-4

 **KEY QUOTES**

Under the Old Covenant spiritual blessings were conveyed largely by the concrete forms of religion in the ceremonial law; abstract teaching was at a minimum. Under the New Covenant, these spiritual blessings are conveyed largely by the abstract teachings of religion; concrete forms, such as the sacraments of Baptism and the Lord's Supper, are at a minimum.[1]

Richard Gray

(The New Covenant) is more spiritual, not only in that the types and ceremonies of the Old Testament are done away, but also in that the revelation itself is more inward and spiritual. What was then made known objectively, is now, to a greater extent, written on the heart. (Heb. 8:8–11.).[2]

Charles Hodge

---

[1] "A Comparison Between The Old Covenant And The New Covenant" Westminster Theological Journal Nov. 1941 p.12
[2] Systematic Theology p.376.

KEY QUESTIONS

1. Why should Christians be baptised?

2. What is wrong with sprinkling an infant?

3. What truths does baptism illustrate?

4. Should someone who is not baptised be a member of an assembly?

TOPIC 3 –
Bread and Wine

!

Key Points

- The bread and wine represent the body and blood of the Lord Jesus.

- The bread and wine are only emblems and, if partaken, do not confer any spiritual benefit on the participant.

- The bread and wine illustrate that God through the death of Christ has supplied the means of and support for spiritual life.

- The Lord's Supper should be partaken by an assembly gathering on the first day of the week.

Introduction

The bread and wine represent the body and blood of the Lord Jesus. The first occasion when bread and wine were used with this in mind was in the Upper Room before Calvary. This is commonly called the Last Supper because it was the Lord Jesus' last meal with His disciples before He died. It was not an ordinary meal. It was the Passover that commemorated Israel's deliverance from Egypt. After the Passover lamb had been eaten however the Lord took bread and wine and asked His disciples to take these emblems as a reminder of Him after He had gone.

As noted in the first chapter there may be symbolic acts as well as symbolic objects. Eating bread and drinking the cup are acts which symbolises our dependence on Christ and our nourishment by his life and death. The bread and wine are symbolic objects. They represent His body and blood. Whereas baptism and head covering are acts undertaken by individuals, the Breaking of Bread is a corporate act. The names given in scripture for these collective acts of remembrance are the Lord's Supper (1 Cor 11:20) and the Breaking of Bread (Acts 2:42). Other names used in Christendom such as Mass, the Eucharist and Communion do not appear in scripture.

The Symbolism of the Emblems

Whereas baptism involves a single liquid element (water) the Lord's Supper involves a solid (bread) and a liquid (wine). The bread and wine parallel the body and blood of Christ. The Lord Jesus made this explicit when He inaugurated the Lord's Supper before He went to the cross; see e.g. Luke 22:19, 20. Care should be taken to notice that not every cup referred to at the Last Supper is a reference to the cup which is used as a memorial of the Lord's death. There were cups used in the Passover meal and one of them is mentioned in Luke 22:14-18 where the Lord uses it to remind the disciples that the symbolism of the Passover will only be fully realised when His kingdom is set up on earth. Thereafter however He took a loaf and another cup and instituted the Lord's Supper which has been observed by the Church to this day.

In interpreting this pair of symbols it is necessary to bear in mind that the phrase "breaking of bread" in the Lord's time had an everyday meaning. Before eating a meal the host would break bread and give thanks e.g. Matt. 14:19; 15:36; Mk. 6:41; 8:6; Lk. 24:30; Acts 27:35. The act of breaking bread was the means by which the host distributed the food. Jewish custom was to allow the head of the house or the host give thanks for the food and then to distribute it to the guests. When considering the significance of breaking of bread it should be remembered that the apostles saw it as a religious "meal". It is called the "Lord's Supper" in contrast to ordinary meals (1 Cor 11:20, 21). The word "supper" (*deipnon*) is the common word in scripture for a meal or the main meal of the day (see e.g. Lk. 14:12; John 13:2, 4). If the breaking of bread signifies the provision of food to the participants in an ordinary meal it is suggested that when we break bread at the Lord's Supper the same idea is being stressed.

The bread and wine teach that the life and death of the Lord Jesus is necessary for spiritual life as physical food is necessary for natural life. Bread is an almost universal symbol of that which nourishes life. The bible uses the expression the "staff of bread"[8] (e.g. Lev. 26:26) to show how bread supports life. The Lord did not fill the cup with water as a symbol of that which supports life even although water is used elsewhere in scripture as a symbol of that which sustains life. Instead He chose wine. This no doubt was because of its colour. Red wine is a vivid symbol of blood. The Lord taught "this cup is the new testament in My blood" (Lk 22:21). The word testament or covenant simply describes an arrangement between two parties involving mutual obligations. At Sinai Jehovah gave Israel the Law and promised that if they kept it He would bless them (Ex 19 and 20). This Covenant is called in the N.T. the "Old" Covenant in contrast to the "New" Covenant. Israel had been promised a "New Covenant" (Jer. 31:31) which would supersede the Covenant of Law. Its main feature was that the Lord would forgive sins permanently and He would give the power to live for God (Jer. 31:33). This promise was realised with the death of Christ which enabled sin to be dealt with finally and completely. As Paul explains in 2 Corinthians the gift of the Spirit enables believers to live for God in a way that was impossible under the Law. Although many insist that the New Covenant has not come into effect it is clear from the Lord's words in Matt. 26:28 (Luke 22:21), Hebrews 8:1-9:28 and 2 Cor. 3:6-18 that the Church today enjoys the spiritual blessing of the New Covenant i.e. forgiveness of sin and power to live for God. Israel will receive the temporal and physical blessings promised to her under the New Covenant when Christ comes to reign. The cup "is the New Covenant" in the sense that it is a symbol of the New Covenant (sometimes called the "New Testament"). His blood had to be shed in order to enable God to forgive our sins and for the Spirit to enter the life. The cup therefore symbolises the fact that in order for God to provide the blessings of the New Covenant to the church the Lord Jesus had to die for sin.

Although scripture speaks of the "cup" and not the wine nothing turns on this distinction. The cup represents the wine that it contains. This is an example of what is called metonymy. Thus the prodigal son in Luke 15:18 and 21 says "I have sinned against heaven" meaning I have sinned against the One who inhabits heaven. Heaven by metonymy means God. We might say "Westminster has passed a law". Westminster is an area of London where the Palace of Westminster is situated. By metonymy Westminster stands for the Parliament situated there. Thus the cup represents the wine which it holds. No commandment is given

---

[8] Possibly the source of the description of bread as the staff of life.

as to the type or design of the cup save (as we shall see) that it should be large enough to supply all present.

The Significance of the Emblems

We have seen that bread symbolises His body. If we break the bread, does the act of "breaking" symbolise the breaking of the Lord's body? This does not seem likely. While the Lord's body was marred it was never "broken". Scripture explicitly teaches that no bone of Him was broken (John 19:36). While His skin was broken it goes too far to say that breaking a loaf of bread in two has a direct parallel to the Lord's physical sufferings. It is better to interpret the act as symbolic of His spiritual work on the cross. Thus the symbolism of breaking bread draws its meaning from an ordinary Jewish meal and symbolises the fact that His life and death impart life and nourishment to His people. The words "this is my body which is broken for you" (1 Cor. 11:24) should therefore be interpreted as a reference to the bread being broken so that each disciple could feed on the common provision (see above).[9]

If the cup is a symbol of the Lord Jesus' blood what is the significance of blood itself? In scripture blood is symbolic of life. Thus in the O.T. blood was treated as the life force of the animal (Lev. 17:11a). When in the sacrifices an animal was slain as an offering its blood was then shed by the priest and he would then offer it as the emblem of death (Lev. 17:11b; Heb. 9:22). There is no saving merit in blood as such i.e. in the chemical compound of plasma, platelets, white cells etc. The meaning and purpose of blood in connection with the offerings is to symbolise the death of the sacrifice. Thus when scripture speaks of the "precious blood" of Christ (1 Peter 1:19) our attention is being drawn to His sacrificial death and its infinite value. Though there is another sense in which His actual blood was precious (because everything about the Lord was precious) that is not the point Peter is making. Thus when we read in Rev. 7:14 of those whose robes were made white in the "blood of the Lamb" we are not thinking of actual blood (which stains) but the death of Christ (which cleanses). Seeing this resolves the need

---

[9] It should also be noted that most translations (e.g. R.V., J.N.D., ESV) drop the word "broken" in 1 Corinthians 11:24 because of a lack of reliable manuscript evidence. They read "this is my body which is for you". If the word "broken" is not in the original text the meaning is simply that the bread symbolished His body given in death on the cross. This would agree with Luke's account of the Lord's words - "this is My body which is given for you" (Lk. 22:19).

to agonise over the fact that His blood was shed <u>after</u> He had died (John 19:33, 34). He had already cried "finished" thus completing the work of atonement, propitiation and reconciliation. This would also save us from the superstitious veneration of relics. In St Basil Chapel in Bruges the Roman Catholics worship a phial said to contain a cloth stained with the blood of the Lord Jesus.

The Substance of the Emblems

The substance or composition of the emblems has generated huge controversy over the years. The Roman Catholics believe that the bread and wine are by some miraculous process turned into the actual body and blood of Christ. This doctrine is called "transubstantiation". Other denominations hold a variation on this theme called "consubstantiation". The root of the controversy is whether the words "this is my body" and "this is my blood" (Lk. 22:19, 20) are to be interpreted literally. If the Lord meant these words literally He was holding parts of His own body at the Last Supper? The sensible way to look at these words is to understand them as figures of speech. The Lord said "I am the door" – He did not mean that He was a real door! Because they believe in transubstantiation Roman Catholics actually worship the wafer and cup as if they were the actual body and blood of Christ. They also re-offer the body of Christ on the altar and thus deny the finality of Christ's death.

The Status of the Emblems

The Roman Catholics believe that taking the "sacraments" (the wafer and the cup) communicates grace to the participant. For this reason they perform the "Mass" at the bedsides of dying people so that when they die they are fit to be accepted by God. In this connection they misapply the Lord's teachings in John 6:53-56 when He said, "Whoso eateth my flesh, and drinketh my blood, hath eternal life" They understand this to refer to the bread and wine taken at the Mass or Communion. It is clear however that He is not speaking of the emblems used at the Lord's Supper which had not yet been instituted. He is speaking about Himself as the "Bread of Life" (vv35, 48) and His words are a figure of speech designed to show the disciples their need to feed on Him through forgiveness and communion. No earthly symbol however can alter the spiritual state of the participant. Salvation is not received through emblems. Salvation is by grace through faith.

The Sharing of the Emblems
Scripture envisages one loaf and one cup. The point is that we all share together in the one provision. Thus in symbol we declare that though we are many we all share in one common provision made by the life and death of Christ.

The primary meaning of the phrase "breaking bread" is the physical act of breaking bread. In the context of an everyday meal the host would break bread. The purpose of breaking bread or whatever other type of food was being eaten, was to distribute the food and enable others to take a piece of bread ("as he sat at meat with them, he took bread, and blessed *it*, and brake, and gave to them", Lk 24:30). In the context of the Lord's Supper it also bears this meaning ("He took bread, and gave thanks, and brake *it*", Lk. 22:20). Since however the Lord's Supper is not an ordinary meal designed to satisfy bodily needs, the expression has a symbolic meaning as well. The breaking of bread and drinking of the cup signifies the spiritual provision made in the life and death of Christ.

At the Lord's Supper the Lord broke the bread and handed it out to the company. After the commencement of the Church there is no indication that any one took over His role at the Lord's Supper and acted as a host in giving thanks on behalf of others and dispensing the emblems. Instead scripture uses language that suggests that the act of breaking bread is a collective activity e.g. "the bread which we break" (1 Cor. 10:16) and "the disciples came together to break bread" (Acts 20:7). This may reflect the unwillingness of the early church to arrogate the role of host to one of their number. The breaking of bread properly understood involves each believer breaking a morsel from the loaf. It is a matter of convenience how this is done. Some assemblies arrange matters so that the whole loaf passes from hand to hand with each believer breaking off a morsel. Others permit one of their number to split the loaf after giving of thanks so that others may take their morsel more easily. Provided this is not thought to be some official act no harm is done. In Christendom it is the preserve of the priest as opposed to the laity to handle the emblems but no such teaching is found in scripture.

The Separation of the Emblems
The Lord might have chosen to be remembered for His humanity alone or His death alone. In choosing both bread and wine, He chose to be remembered for both His life and death. In life the blood and body co-exist. In sacrifice the blood

is separated from the body. The fact that there is a separate emblem for His death suggests therefore that His life has been given. It is sometimes said that the words "this cup is the new testament in my blood which is shed (or *being poured out*) for you" (Luke 22:20) indicate that the shedding of the Lord's blood is to be commemorated by a symbolic pouring of wine. This is a possible reading of this verse. Much depends on whether He was actually pouring wine from the cup as He spoke. The words "poured out" are in the present tense and this may imply that the wine was being poured. This reading however has two difficulties. First if it is assumed that the verse is speaking about wine being poured out, the cup would as a result be emptied. But Matthew 26:27 shows that they were commanded to drink from this cup. That would have been impossible if the cup had been poured out. Second the nearest object of the verb "pour" is not "this cup" but "my blood". The words "being poured out" more naturally refer to His blood poured out in sacrifice. The pouring out of blood is an established figure of speech in the O.T. for sacrificial death; see Lev. 4:7, 18, 25 and 30; 8:15; 9:9. The present tense would then be an example of the "futuristic present" tense. Here are some examples. In John 14:3 the Lord said "And if I go and prepare a place for you, <u>I am coming again</u>". In John 20:17 He said "...go to my brethren, and say unto them, <u>I am ascending</u> to my Father...". Although His second coming and ascension were future events when He spoke, He spoke of them as though they were happening in the present. Thus when He said that the cup was being poured out for you, He was referring to His sacrificial death which He would accomplish on the morrow and which was typified in the cup. What then did the Lord mean when He said "this do as oft as ye drink it" (1st Cor. 11:25)? What was he asking them to do every time they drank the cup? There are a number of possibilities. The most likely is that they had to give thanks.

The Sequence of the Emblems

It is noteworthy that the Lord first broke the bread and then took the wine. Not the other way around. This I suggest indicates that the incarnation and life of Christ was a precursor to His death. His sinless life was the foundation of His sacrificial death. That is not to say that the bread is not linked to His death since the Lord says that it signifies His body "given for you" (Lk. 22:19). In 1 Corinthians ch 10:16 it is interesting to see that the order is reversed and Paul speaks first of the cup and then of the bread. I believe that Paul is seeking to draw attention to the fact that the believers in Corinth who had become divided and antagonistic to one another had lost sight of the fact that through the Lord's death they had been united together.

The Singularity of the Emblems
A single loaf and a single cup are important symbols of the essential unity of God's people (1 Cor 10:17). While a single loaf and cup pose no problem when the assembly is small or medium size, problems can arise in large gatherings. If there is one loaf and one cup the eating and drinking can take a long time. I personally feel that this should not be a deterrent. These symbolic acts are after all the main reason for the gathering. It is possible to bake a large loaf and if necessary the cup can be replenished. While we should not be too hung up about ritual, the symbolism of one loaf and one cup is important.

Some denominations use wafers and each participant is given a wafer rather than taking a morsel of bread. This is not the scriptural pattern. Likewise some use individual cups for each participant. This completely destroys the symbolism of scripture.

The Singularity of the Supper
Care should be taken to distinguish those occasions when the disciples "broke bread" to remember the Lord (e.g. Luke 22:19) and those where the "breaking of bread" was an ordinary meal (see e.g. Luke 24:35; Acts 27:35). There are two occasions in scripture where the same expression "breaking of bread" is used in the same passage to mean different things. In Acts ch 2:42-46 we read that the church at Jerusalem -

"continued stedfastly in the apostles' doctrine and fellowship, and **in breaking of bread**, and in prayers. [43] And fear came upon every soul: and many wonders and signs were done by the apostles. [44] And all that believed were together, and had all things common; [45] And sold their possessions and goods, and parted them to all *men*, as every man had need. [46] And they, continuing daily with one accord in the temple, and **breaking bread from house to house**, did eat their meat with gladness and singleness of heart,

In Acts 20:7-11 we read

[7] And upon the first *day* of the week, when **the disciples came together to break bread**, Paul preached unto them, ready to depart on the morrow; and continued his speech until midnight. [8] And there were many lights in

the upper chamber, where they were gathered together. [9] And there sat in a window a certain young man named Eutychus, being fallen into a deep sleep: and as Paul was long preaching, he sunk down with sleep, and fell down from the third loft, and was taken up dead. [10] And Paul went down, and fell on him, and embracing *him* said, Trouble not yourselves; for his life is in him. [11] When he therefore was come up again, **and had broken bread, and eaten**, and talked a long while, even till break of day, so he departed.

In these passages the first use of "breaking of bread" refers to the Lord's Supper and the second to an ordinary meal. The context in Acts 2:46 makes it clear that they did not celebrate the Lord's Supper "from house to house" but that the early Christians initially met in the temple and ate their meals together in the believers' homes. Likewise in Troas in Acts 20 the disciples met to have the Lord's Supper and Paul then spoke at length to them. After the incident with Eutychus they "broke bread" again. The words "broken bread and eaten" indicate that an ordinary meal is in view.

The Simplicity of the Supper

Despite the elaborate ceremonies fashioned by Christendom, the Lord's Supper is (or should be) the model of simplicity. There is no rule as to how long the gathering should be. No rule as to whether it should be in the morning or evening. No rule that it must be in a church building. No rule that we must sing. Whatever arrangements are made must be "unto edifying" (1 Cor. 14:26). Some with good reason prefer to make it the first observance of the Lord's Day. However we must recognise that scripture makes it plain that the Christians broke bread in Corinth and Troas in the evening. No doubt the fact that these were pagan cities in which Sunday was just another working day may have affected that arrangement. In Africa today some assemblies preach the gospel and have Sunday school in the morning before it gets too hot. Hence they break bread after these meetings.

Hymn books are a valuable aid to worship but we may still remember the Lord in the absence of hymn books. In my estimation if it is not possible to obtain bread or wine, it is still possible to remember the Lord. In some parts of the world, notably sub-Saharan Africa, bread and wine are not local commodities because barley, wheat and vines do not grow there. If they cannot buy bread or wine they use a close equivalent such as wafers or coloured water. In our own country some assemblies do not use real wine because of the problem it can pose reformed alcoholics.

The Sanction for the Supper

Breaking bread is not an option for the believer. The Lord Jesus said "this do in remembrance of Me" (1 Cor. 11:24). When we break bread we obey Him.

The Sunday Supper

Whereas baptism is a single act and does not require to be repeated, the breaking of the bread and the drinking of the cup is a weekly act of remembrance. It appears from the Acts of the Apostles that the disciples were in the habit of remembering the Lord Jesus on the first day of the week (Acts 20:7). Since Sunday was the day the Lord rose from the dead it makes sense that they should choose to remember the Lord on that day. Most of the early Christians were Jews and the last day of the week, the Sabbath, was the day when they traditionally met. The significance of the Sabbath is the commemoration of God's rest after the work of creation. Christians were instructed by Paul to stop observing the Sabbath (Col. 2:16). Thus although there is no passage of scripture that teaches us explicitly that we should break bread on the first day of the week it is clear that apostolic practice was to break bread on Sunday. This fits with the fact that the Lord rose from the dead on Sunday morning[10] (Matt. 28:1; Mark 16:2). The Church of Scotland, Free Church and other denominations have a "Communion Sunday" every 3 or 6 months. By contrast the Catholics and Anglicans celebrate Mass constantly. It is taken at funerals, weddings, hospital bedsides etc. There are private masses, public masses - confusion reigns!

The Sign of the Supper

Whereas baptism is a personal testimony by an individual Christian, the Breaking of Bread is a corporate testimony by the church. We nowhere read of people celebrating the Lord's Supper on their own. In the Upper Room before Calvary it was observed by the apostles (minus Judas who had left by that stage to betray the Lord) and the Lord. These apostles were the founding members of the church

---

[10] We call Sunday "the Lord's Day". The expression "the Lord's Day" is only used once in the N.T. in Rev. 1:10. Some think that the phrase is a reference to the future "Day of the Lord" when the Lord returns in judgment but for grammatical and contextual reasons it seems likely that John is singling out a day and it seems probable that this was the first day of the week. The early church certainly thought so since "the Lord's Day" is a common term for Sunday in literature from the second century.

in Jerusalem. Thereafter every occasion on which we read of the Lord's Supper we find the disciples meeting collectively to break bread. Not all Christians see things this way. I have read of pioneering missionaries from the assemblies who broke bread on the Lord's Day in the bush in Central Africa far from any assembly. Without wishing to be critical and while acknowledging the right of Christians to live in the light of their own conscience, the present writer sees no precedent or liberty in scripture for such a practice.

The Summation of the Supper

In summary when an assembly breaks bread and drinks the cup the brethren should offer thanks, as He gave thanks at that first Supper. Their thanksgivings should be sincere and scriptural. They need not be long. Sisters should also give thanks. But they should not do so audibly (1 Cor. 14:28; 1 Tim. 2:11, 12). In taking the emblems the assembly is reminded that they are sustained by Him. The bread reminds them of His holy humanity and perfect life. The cup reminds them of His atoning death. As they break bread they do so "till He come" (1 Cor. 11:26).

KEY SCRIPTURES

^{26} And as they were eating, Jesus took bread, and blessed *it*, and brake *it*, and gave *it* to the disciples, and said, Take, eat; this is my body. ^{27} And he took the cup, and gave thanks, and gave *it* to them, saying, Drink ye all of it[11]; ^{28} For this is my blood of the new testament, which is shed for many for the remission of sins. ^{29} But I say unto you, I will not drink henceforth of this fruit of the vine, until that day when I drink it new with you in my Father's kingdom.

Mt 26:26-29

^{22} And as they did eat, Jesus took bread, and blessed, and brake *it*, and gave to them, and said, Take, eat: this is my body. ^{23} And he took the cup, and when he had given thanks, he gave *it* to them: and they all drank of it. ^{24} And he said unto them, This is my blood of the new testament, which is shed for many. ^{25} Verily I say unto you, I will drink no more of the fruit of the vine, until that day that I drink it new in the kingdom of God.

Mk 14:22-25

^{14} And when the hour was come, he sat down, and the twelve apostles with him. ^{15} And he said unto them, With desire I have desired to eat this passover with you before I suffer: ^{16} For I say unto you, I will not any more eat thereof, until it be fulfilled in the kingdom of God. ^{17} And he took the cup, and gave thanks, and said, Take this, and divide *it* among yourselves: ^{18} For I say unto you, I will not drink of the fruit of the vine, until the kingdom of God shall come. ^{19} And he took bread, and gave thanks, and brake *it*, and gave unto them, saying, This is my body which is given for you: this do in remembrance of me. ^{20} Likewise also the cup after supper, saying, This cup *is* the new testament in my blood, which is shed for you.

Lk 22:14-20

---

[11] "Each of you drink from it", N.L.T.; "Drink of it, all of you," E.S.V.

KEY SCRIPTURES

¹⁶ The cup of blessing which we bless, is it not the communion of the blood of Christ? The bread which we break, is it not the communion of the body of Christ? ¹⁷ For we *being* many are one bread, *and* one body: for we are all partakers of that one bread.

1 Cor. 10:16-17

²³ For I have received of the Lord that which also I delivered unto you, That the Lord Jesus the *same* night in which he was betrayed took bread: ²⁴ And when he had given thanks, he brake *it*, and said, Take, eat: this is my body, which is broken for you: this do in remembrance of me. ²⁵ After the same manner also *he took* the cup, when he had supped, saying, This cup is the new testament in my blood: this do ye, as oft as ye drink *it*, in remembrance of me. ²⁶ For as often as ye eat this bread, and drink this cup, ye do shew the Lord's death till he come.

1 Cor. 11:23-26

This is my body, which *is* for you: this do in remembrance of me... 1 Cor. 11:24 (JND)

1 Cor. 11:24 (JND)

KEY QUOTES

Sweet feast of love divine!
'Tis grace that makes us free
To feed upon this bread and wine,
In memory, Lord, of Thee.

Here every welcome guest
Waits, Lord, from Thee to learn
The secrets of Thy Father's breast,
And all Thy grace discern.

But if this glimpse of love
Is so divinely sweet,
What will it be, O Lord, above,
Thy gladdening smile to meet—

Here conscience ends its strife,
And faith delights to prove
The sweetness of the bread of life,
The fullness of Thy love.

Thy blood that flowed for sin,
In symbol here we see,
And feel the blessèd pledge within,
That we are loved of Thee.

To see Thee face to face,
Thy perfect likeness wear,
And all Thy ways of wondrous grace
Through endless years declare!

Edward Denny

The effect of the sacrifices under the Mosaic economy was to bring "iniquity to remembrance" (Num. 5:15); the design of the breaking of bread and drinking of the cup is to bring the hearts of the partakers to the realisation of what Christ is to them as Lord and Saviour, and what they are to Him through His redeeming blood.[12]

W E Vine

The purpose of the institution is seen as being threefold. First the Lord said "this do in remembrance of Me". All that relates to His blessed Person is involved in this remembrance. Then it is a proclamation. "Ye proclaim the Lord's death till He come". All the love and suffering and blessing that is involved in the death of our Lord is in this proclamation. The third truth expressed is the unity of the body of Christ.[33]

Norman Crawford

---

[12] The Collected Writings of W E Vine (vol. 5) GTP p.165.
[13] Gathering Unto His Name (GTP) p.57.

??? KEY QUESTIONS

1. What do the bread and wine symbolise?

2. What benefit is there in eating the bread and drinking the cup at the Lord's Supper?

3. Who should break bread and drink the cup and how frequently?

4. List three similarities and three dissimilarities between the Last Supper and the Lord's Supper.

TOPIC 4 – The Head Covering

Key Points

- The purpose of the covered head of the woman is to illustrate creational truths laid down by God in the Garden of Eden and which persist to the present day.

- Although man and woman are equal in God's eyes, they fulfil different roles and the head covering illustrates the difference God has placed between the sexes.

- The uncovered head of the man is as important as the covered head of the woman.

- Men are expected to have short hair and women to have long hair.

INTRODUCTION

The assemblies' insistence on the need for women to cover their heads in the assembly gatherings has become one of their distinctive doctrinal characteristics. In days gone by women from many denominational backgrounds covered their heads in church. But this is no longer so. Even other groups whose beliefs are close to the assemblies either frown on headcovering or leave it to the conscience of the women. This chapter will look at the issue of headcovering and explore its scriptural basis and assess whether there is any reason to abandon it or relegate it to an issue of conscience.

There is only one passage that deals with the topic in the N.T. This is 1 Cor. 11:3-16. If doctrinal importance can be measured by the amount of space devoted to it, headcovering is important. It is a lengthy section. Crucially however the principles on which the passage rests lie at the foundations of Christianity and Judaism. A great deal is at stake. This is not some obscure argument about an obscure passage.

INTERPRETATION
V.3 "But I would have you know, that the head of every man is Christ; and the head of the woman *is* the man; and the head of Christ *is* God."
In everyday speech the word "head" is used to refer to the physical head or someone who has authority over others. Thus we speak about the "head" of an organization and "head teachers". It is evident here that the word "head" does not refer to a human head. The passage teaches that Christ is the "head" of every man. In other words He is in a position of authority. The words translated "man" in verse 3 may signify either a male or a person. Since he speaks very generally of "every man" in the first part of the verse this indicates that Paul has all people of both sexes in view. Thus all people are subject to the headship of Christ. In the second part of the verse the word "man" is placed alongside "woman". Paul is obviously contrasting males and females. To complicate things the word for "man" (*aner*) can mean "husband" and the word for "woman" (*gune*) can mean either woman or "wife". It seems likely that he meant "woman". Otherwise all unmarried women (the young, the single and the widowed) would fall outside the scope of the headship of man and be covered only by the headship of Christ. It should be noted that being the "head" does not imply superiority since God (the Father) has headship or authority over Christ though equal with Him (see Phil. 2.6).

V.4 "Every man praying or prophesying, having *his* head covered, dishonoureth his head."
Only human heads can be "covered" so the word "head" in the first part of the verse refers to the human head unlike v.3. The passage introduces the theme of honour and dishonour. Paul teaches that it is disgraceful to pray or prophesy with a covered head. We might wonder why. The remainder of the passage supplies the answer. Dishonour arises because he is wearing a symbol of submission that ought to be worn by the woman. Although the Father is the head of the Son, the Lord Jesus did not wear a head covering as a token of His submission. Likewise the man does not cover his head as a token of his submission to Christ. The head covering is only required as between the sexes because the teaching of this passage is designed to deal with headship between men and women.

V.5 "But every woman that prayeth or prophesieth with *her* head uncovered dishonoureth her head: for that is even all one as if she were shaven."
This verse parallels verse 4. As verse 4 deals with the man's physical head so this verse deals with the woman's physical head. Although it is true that her uncovered head in a sense dishonours Christ and the man, her spiritual heads, it is unlikely the apostle had this in mind since the dishonoured head is likened to a shaven head. A woman without her head covered is "even all one" (equivalent to) a woman with a shaved head. Paul draws a parallel between a head with no covering and a head with no hair. It is clear from this verse that Paul distinguishes between the head covering worn on the head and a woman's natural covering namely the hair that grows from her head. Where the woman is praying and prophesying is not stated. Nor does he deal with the restriction on women praying and prophesying until 14:34.

V.6 "For if the woman be not covered, let her also be shorn: but if it be a shame for a woman to be shorn or shaven, let her be covered."
He restates the point by saying that an uncovered head is as shameful as a "shorn" or "shaven" head. "Shorn" translates *keiro* the word used in Acts 8.32 to translate Isa. 53.7 "a sheep before her *shearers*". It is also used in Acts 18.18 where we read "having *shorn* his head in Cenchrea: for he had a vow" (cf. Acts 21.24-26; Num. 6.1-21). What he is saying is, if a woman has no head covering this is as shameful as if her natural covering had been removed by cutting her hair short or shaving off all her hair.

V.7 "For a man indeed ought not to cover *his* head, forasmuch as he is the image and glory of God: but the woman is the glory of the man."
Paul now goes to the root of his teaching and explains why head covering is necessary. Man is the "image" of God. This is what God stated in the beginning (Gen. 1:26, 27; 9:6). Man procreated in his image (Gen. 5:3). In other words when He made man God imparted to him some of his essential features. Obviously this did not include the essentials of deity such as omniscience and omnipotence but He gave him a sense of morality, spirituality and an appreciation of aesthetics. He is God's "glory" in that he was made for the purpose of honouring Him and was the crown of creation; see 1Tim.2.13. By contrast Eve was formed by God from Adam to assist Adam. Paul's purpose is

not to deny that women were also made in the image of God but to stress that woman was made to bring glory to man.

V.8 "For the man is not of the woman; but the woman of the man."
Adam came first. Adam was created from the dust. Eve was later formed from Adam's rib.

V.9 "Neither was the man created for the woman; but the woman for the man."
God made Eve for Adam (Gen. 2.18). This state of affairs does not imply inferiority since Scripture treats men and women as of equal worth but it does indicate the purpose for which woman was made was different from that for which man was made in some fundamental respects. It may be that the rise of evolution and the scorn poured by many so called theologians on the book of Genesis explains why headship is no longer taken seriously.

V.10 "For this cause ought the woman to have power on *her* head because of the angels."
Paul returns to the issue in hand. Headship is not only a symbol of the relationship God has ordained between the sexes but it also has a didactic role. Although he does not specify what role angels have in his argument it is probable that he intends us to understand that they learn from the acknowledgement of headship. The word "power" means "authority". What Paul means is that the head covering is a symbol of authority.

V.11 "Nevertheless neither is the man without the woman, neither the woman without the man, in the Lord."
Here he seeks to prevent any misunderstanding of his argument. Despite his headship man is not in a relationship of dominance but one of interdependence with woman. They ought to honour and respect each other. This ideal is fully realised by those who are "in the Lord".

V.12 "For as the woman *is* of the man, even so *is* the man also by the woman; but all things of God."
Although Eve came from Adam, all men ever since have been born of a woman; so man cannot claim he does not need the woman or look down on women. Although we were all born of women everyone ultimately owes their existence to the Creator God.

V.13 "Judge in yourselves: is it comely that a woman pray unto God uncovered?"
His arguments thus far have been based on creatorial order and the need to instruct the angelic creation. Here he argues that intuition has a role to play. He teaches that it is not natural for a woman to pray without a covering. This goes back to man and woman being made in the image of God. He has placed a sense of what is normal and proper in our hearts and conscience. Some may suppress that sense of what is right and wrong. It may be possessed in varying degrees but it is there.

Vv.14,15 "Doth not even nature itself teach you, that, if a man have long hair, it is a shame unto him? But if a woman have long hair, it is a glory to her: for *her* hair is given her for a covering."
He moves away here from head covering to a connected issue which illustrates the same point. He points out that there is another head covering supplied by nature. That is hair. He observes that women wear long hair and men short hair. He draws the parallel between the fact that women have such a covering whereas men wear short hair. Paul's observation was entirely accurate. In most cultures at that time men had shorter hair than women. Long hair was regarded as effeminate. "Nature" does not refer to a biological difference between sexes but what was normal. Men can grow very long hair so there is no biological reason for the difference. Here Paul is careful to mark that the covering provided by hair is different from the covering placed on the head. The words for "cover" and "uncovered" (vv.4-7) are *katakalyptomai* ("to have on the head") and *akatakaluptos* (not to have on the head). Here the word for "covering" is *peribolaion* which means a covering such as a cloak or veil (e.g. Heb.1.12). The two types of covering should not be confused. Paul uses different language for the covering worn on the head from the hair that grows from the head.

V.16 "But if any man seem to be contentious, we have no such custom, neither the churches of God."
This verse is a hammer blow to those that argue that Paul's argument is meshed in the peculiarities of Corinthians culture.

IMPLEMENTATION
The passage above throws up a variety of questions about how these truths should be put into practice.

What kind of head covering should be worn?

The head covering is not defined other than by its function. Scripture does not prescribe what type of head covering should be worn. As one might expect fashion and cultural norms influence what women wear. In the UK hats are the norm. In other parts of the world veils are the norm. Sisters should not seek to use the symbol of headship as an opportunity to rebel against social norms or as an opportunity to make a "fashion statement". That said, provided the head is covered, it is for each sister to decide in the light of their own conscience what type of covering to wear. Note that it is a head covering not a hair covering. Scripture teaches that a woman should have long hair but there is no requirement in scripture for the head covering to also cover the woman's hair or for that matter for the woman to conceal her hair beneath a head covering. If a sister chooses to wear her hair "up" while wearing the head covering that is a matter of personal preference not command.

Who should wear headcoverings? The Bible teaches that women should wear them. The principles upon which Paul rests his teaching are found in creatorial order. This indicates that ideally all women should wear them when it is appropriate to do so. Thus unsaved daughters should be encouraged by Christian parents to wear head coverings. The first section of 1 Cor. 11 is based on creation. The second section vv17-34 is based on Lordship which in turn is based on salvation. That said only Christians "pray or prophesy" and only Christians see their relationship with one another as "in the Lord" (v11). However in light of the fact that the section is a comprehensive review of mankind's relationship to God and between the sexes, unsaved females should ideally cover their heads. That does not mean that we force unsaved people to wear head coverings if they come to hear the gospel. A bit of common sense is needed. But where we can influence them to do so we should encourage unsaved women to cover their heads and unsaved men to be bare headed at the gatherings.

When is a woman required to cover her head? This has to be decided by the context of ch. 11 since Paul does not state expressly where he has in mind. The preceding section (ch. 10) has to do with everyday life. The succeeding section (11:17) has to do with the assembly gathering. But what about verses 3-16? There are some clues. Paul refers to the need for headcovering when there is prayer or prophesy. This suggests that he is speaking about public prayer since prophesy

(14:29) was a gift the apostle thought was for the edification of the church. Thus although we engage in private prayer at home, prayer along with prophesy was part of church life (1 Cor. 14:6, 15). If headcovering is required for private prayer then the headcoveirng would have to be worn at all times since prayer may be engaged in at all times. But this would not fit with the argument of the passage. Paul refers to the Corinthians sense of public decorum. He refers to "shame" and what is "comely". These words imply that he is speaking about public behaviour. He also states (v16) that his teaching was the practice of "the churches". To my mind these factors indicate that private prayer is not in view and that a sister is not obliged to cover her head at home. Of course there are difficult questions about events which are neither domestic not church gatherings. What should happen at weddings, funerals and events where the word of God is opened or public prayer is offered? In the author's opinion headship should be recognised in these situations. Headship is a creational truth and on that account it is better to give it an expansive rather than a restrictive application in cases of doubt.

Paul proceeds on the assumption that women pray and prophecy in ch 11. Does that not show that it is wrong to require sisters to be silent?
Paul certainly says that if a woman prays or prophesies with her head uncovered she dishonours her head. On the other hand he says in 1 Cor 14:34 that women are to be in silence in the church. See also 1 Tim 2:11, 12. It may be that Paul was aware that women were taking public part in Corinth. This would explain why he dealt with this issue in ch 14. In ch 11 he is dealing with the issue of a woman who is taking part with an uncovered head and deals with her failure to wear the head covering. He does not deal at this stage with the separate question of whether taking audible part in prayer or prophesy is consistent with the truth that the head covering is meant to symbolise. If so he deals with the need for silence as a consequence of the sisters' submission in ch.14. Another possibility is that he is speaking about women praying and prophesying outside the church gatherings like the four daughters of Philip the Evangelist (Acts 21:9). But to my mind that is unlikely since Paul is teaching in this section that there is a general obligation on a woman to wear a symbol of her subjection to the man. This obligation is based on creatorial order. In his teaching about the role of women Paul leans heavily on what can be discerned from creation. In particular he emphasises that females have a supporting role not a dominant role in the relationship between the sexes. Woman was made to support man. Man was not created to support anyone but to

bring glory to God. These creatorial principles are relied on by the apostle to teach both headcovering and the silence of women.

Nearly all Christian leaders and authors today say that this section was only applicable to Corinth or to Greek society in the 1ˢᵗ century. Is that so?
Paul does not give any hint that what he had to say was unique to Corinth or Greek culture. The other great truths he teaches in the epistle such as the holiness of the assembly and the supremacy of love are all universal truths. It should also be noted that when summing up his argument he states in verse 16 "But if any man seem to be contentious, we have no such custom, neither the churches of God." The "we" refers to the apostles and "the churches of God" refers to all other churches at that time which were scattered round the Mediterranean basin in a great variety of different countries including present day Israel, Greece, Italy and Turkey. If all these churches were of the same mind then there was nothing unique about Corinth or Greece. In addition in this section Paul appeals to the order God established in creation which is applicable to all people in all places and times. He refers to "nature" which is that instinct God gives people about what is right and wrong. Although many commentators argue that this is shaped by culture and society I think Paul is indicating that a Christian's innate sense of what is right and proper should lead him to the conclusion that there ought to be a distinction between the sexes in the gatherings of the church and in public service for God.

What does this passage have to teach about hairstyles?
Nothing. Elaborate hairstyles are dealt with by Peter in 1 Peter 3:3 and Paul in 1 Timothy 2:9. What Paul is doing in this passage is contrasting hair length. Paul does not deal with the issue of whether that hair is worn up or down. These are matters for the good sense of the sisters. In my judgment the "braiding" and "plaiting" of 1 Tim 2:9 and 1 Peter 3:3 do not refer to hair that is tied back or pinned up but hair arrangements that are highly elaborate and designed to attract attention.

If the principles in ch 11 are universal why did priests cover their heads in the tabernacle and temple?
It is certainly true that men wore headcoverings in the OT. The High Priest wore

---

4 Although Herod built a Court of the Women no instruction is given in scripture for such a place in connection with the construction of the tabernacle, Solomon's temple or Ezekiel's temple.

a mitre (or turban) and the priests wore bonnets. This practice is also described in the millennial temple in Ezekiel (Ezek. 44:18). It may be that the reason for the change in 1ˢᵗ Corinthians ch 11 is that there were no women priests in the tabernacle and temple.[14] The High Priests and the priests were always males. In the church males and females are both members and women attend occasions of public prayer and preaching. In recognition of this new situation the old obligation of head covering as a sign of the submission of the male priest before God is changed and the female covers her head when in the company of the men. The symbol of the priest's submission to God is now worn by woman in token of her submission to man. Although male Jews today wear prayer shawls over their heads in the synagogue I am not aware of any scriptural precedent for this.

How long should a women's hair be and how short should a man's be?

All that the bible says is that a woman's hair should be long and a man's hair short. These are the opposite ends of a spectrum. Sisters should therefore avoid compromises by cutting their hair so that it is neither short nor long. Although some good sisters are convicted that their hair should be as long as nature allows the bible does not go so far as to say that hair should never be cut. It is equally true that men are not commanded to have their hair as short as it can be. They are not required to shave their heads. The Nazarite vow required the person not to cut their hair (Num. 6:5). Since women could take the vow it seems that uncut hair was part of their vow as it was for men.[15]

It may be thought obvious that "uncut hair" and "long hair" are different things. An African sister can have uncut hair which is short. A British sister can have cut hair and yet it may still be long. We should be slow to judge sisters whose hair is not as long as others. Hair lengths are determined by nature. Some would love to have long hair but their hair does not grow well. It is a great shame that sisters who could have long hair cut it so that it is either of short or medium length. As in all things our guidance should be taken from scripture not the world around us or even the hair styles of other Christians.

---

[15] See Num. 6:2.

INTERACTION

It may be helpful if we look at what Christian writers who are not connected to the assemblies have said about 1 Corinthians 11:3-16. Do their arguments make sense? Here is what Fee and Stuart have to say -

> Paul appeals to the divine order of creation and redemption and establishes the principle that one should do nothing to detract from the glory of God (especially by breaking convention) when the community is at worship (vv7, 10). The specific application however appears to be relative since Paul repeatedly appeals to "practice" or "nature" (vv6, 13-14, 16). This leads us to... ask... "Would this have been an issue for us had we never encountered it in the New Testament documents?" In Western cultures the failure to cover a woman's head (especially her hair) with a full length veil would probably create no difficulties at all. In fact if she were to literally obey the text in most American churches she would thereby abuse the spirit of the text by drawing attention to herself.[16]

Fee and Stuart's argument ignores the fact that headship is based on creatorial order. The principles laid down in the Garden of Eden were established long before any cultures had developed. In verse 16 Paul teaches that all the churches of God (whatever culture they were in) practiced headcovering. Sometimes scripture expects us to stand out from our culture. Thus for example if society regards homosexuality as acceptable it does not follow that the bible must be interpreted so as to follow contemporary social norms. MacArthur takes a similar line to Fee and Stuart and says -

> The apostle is not laying down an absolute law for women to wear veils or coverings in all churches for all time but is declaring that the symbols of the divinely established male and female roles are to be genuinely honoured in every culture... there is nothing spiritual about wearing or not wearing a covering. But manifesting rebellion against God's order was wrong. [17]

[16] How to Read the Bible for All Its Worth (Zondervan) Fee and Stuart p 83.
[17] The MacArthur Bible Commentary (Nelson) p. 1588
[3] p. 1603.

Again it must be stressed that Paul's argument is not based on Corinthian culture. He appeals to "nature" and refers to the practice of all the churches. It is very hard to understand why Paul's teaching is not meant to apply "in all churches for all time". It is also hard to understand why later in the book MacArthur feels able to he argue that women should be silent in the church.[18] The silence of the sisters rests on the same creational principles as headship. Another well-known Christian author Warren Wiersbe argues as follows -

> The woman's long hair is her glory, and it is given to her "instead of a covering" (literal translation). In other words, if local custom does not dictate a head-covering, her long hair can be that covering. I do not think that Paul meant for all women in every culture to wear a shawl for a head-covering; but he did expect them to use their long hair as a covering and as a symbol of their submission to God's order. This is something that every woman can do. In my ministry in different parts of the world, I have noticed that the basic principle of headship applies in every culture; but the means of demonstrating it differs from place to place. The important thing is the submission of the heart to the Lord and the public manifestation of obedience to God's order.[19]

His argument depends on a translation of v15 "her hair is given her instead of a covering"[1] that is not widely accepted. Most translations say "for a covering" (A.V., NKJV, E.S.V., ASV, NASV, NRSV), or "as a covering" (N.I.V. NLT) which comes to the same thing. As we have noticed the section makes a distinction between the covering worn on the head and the covering of hair supplied by nature. The ring supplied by nature illustrates the general truth of headship.

---

[19] The Bible Exposition Commentary (Victor Books) p. 604.
[20] Young's Literal Translation; cf. the New Translation "the long hair is given to her in lieu of a veil".

INVIGORATION

My impression is that many who are in fellowship have little appreciation of how clear the word of God is about headship. They feel embarrassed or even apologetic about the insistence on head covering. There is nothing to be apologetic about. Although there are occasions other than assembly gatherings where it is not crystal clear what should be done I would encourage sisters to err on the side of caution in the matter of head covering. If in doubt "cover up". God's glory is at stake and man's opinions do not matter. It is sadly the case that many sisters in the assemblies have short hair. I am certain that in most cases that this is not deliberate rebellion. I am also certain that most Christian women sincerely desire to obey the word of God.

KEY QUESTIONS

1. What does the uncovered head of the man symbolize?

2. What does the covered head of the woman symbolize?

3. When should a man have an uncovered head and a woman a covered head?

4. What does the bible have to say about hair length?